TECH IN THE TRENCHES

# Strategic Inventions of World War II

Jeri Freedman

Cavendish Square
New York

Published in 2016 by Cavendish Square Publishing, LLC
243 5th Avenue, Suite 136, New York, NY 10016



First Edition



CPSIA Compliance Information: Batch #CW16CSQ



Cataloging-in-Publication Data

Freedman, Jeri.
Strategic inventions of World War II / by Jeri Freedman.
p. cm. — (Tech in the trenches)
Includes index.
ISBN 978-1-5026-1026-3 (hardcover) ISBN 978-1-5026-1027-0 (ebook)
1. World War, 1939-1945 — Juvenile literature. 2. World War, 1939-1945 — Equipment and supplies — Juvenile literature. 3. Military weapons — History — 20th century — Juvenile literature. I. Freedman, Jeri. II. Title.
D743.7 F74 2016
813'.54—d23

Editorial Director: David McNamara
Editor: Kristen Susienka
Copy Editor: Nathan Heidelberger
Art Director: Jeffrey Talbot
Designer: Alan Sliwinski/Amy Greenan
Senior Production Manager: Jennifer Ryder-Talbot
Production Editor: Renni Johnson
Photo Research: J8 Media

The photographs in this book are used by permission and through the courtesy of: Mikael Damkier/Shutterstock.com, cover; PhotoQuest/Getty Images, 4; SSPL/Getty Images, 9; US Army/The LIFE Picture Collection/Getty Images, 11; Everett Historical/Shutterstock.com, 14; Keystone/Getty Images, 18; Everett Historical/Shutterstock.com, 24; Hulton Archive/Getty Images, 26; Hulton Archive/Getty Images, 30; ullstein bild/ullstein bild via Getty Images, 32; Boyer/Roger Viollet/Getty Images, 36; Hulton Archive/Getty Images, 40; NINUN/Shutterstock.com, 43; ullstein bild/ullstein bild via Getty Images, 46; Universal History Archive/Getty Images, 49; Fouad A. Saad/Shutterstock.com, 51; Everett Historical/Shutterstock.com, 54; Roger Viollet/Getty Images, 56; Fox Photos/Getty Images, 59; ullstein bild/ullstein bild via Getty Images, 60; ullstein bild/ullstein bild via Getty Images, 66; Antoine Taveneaux/File:Bletchley Park Bombe4.jpg/Wikimedia Commons, 71; Monty Fresco/Topical Press Agency/Getty Images, 76; Everett Historical/Shutterstock.com, 80; Sovfoto/UIG via Getty Images, 84; Time & Life Pictures/The LIFE Images Collection/Getty Images, 87; Mitglieder der Akaflieg München/Akaflieg München e.V./File:Akaflieg DM 1.jpg/Wikimedia Commons, 90; Underwood Archives/Getty Images, 97; SSPL/Getty Images, 100.

Printed in the United States of America

# CONTENTS

The V-2 rocket, an advanced guided missile developed by the Germans during World War II

INTRODUCTION

# A War to Remember

Many of the great inventions we think of as twenty-first century technology actually have their roots in equipment and devices developed during World War II. Unlike the wars that came before it, World War II was a technological war. It was fought as much in the research laboratories of both the **Axis** and **Allied powers** as on the battlefield. Wartime research and development resulted in completely new types of weapons. Many technologies originally invented for attack or defense developed into some of the most pervasive technologies we use today in peacetime. Jet fighter technology led to jet bombers, but also eventually to commercial airlines that have become a mainstay of modern travel. The development of the atomic bomb led to weapons that still threaten world peace today, but also to nuclear power plants that provide electricity, especially in parts of the world where other sources of fuel are rare. Plastics, developed to replace metal needed for the war effort, are now a ubiquitous part of life, used for everything from food packaging to pipes to medical devices. Antibiotics, first widely used during World War II, are now a necessity of health care. Rockets designed to destroy cities led to spacecraft used to reach the moon, put exploratory robots on other planets, and launch satellites into space. Those satellites, in turn, have changed the way we communicate and increased our understanding of weather and atmospheric changes that affect Earth.

The pace of scientific development during World War II was extraordinary. Prior to the war, many engineers working for companies involved in commercial products were focused on producing new forms of entertainment—moving from radio to television—and making improvements in existing technologies. New ideas like rockets were the realm of science fiction stories written for popular magazines and amateur hobbyists. However, the massive military forces of Germany and Japan in the 1930s, sweeping across Europe and Southeast Asia, respectively, changed all that. Advanced tanks and **artillery**; new types of aircraft and bombs, and the radar to detect them; mechanical **encrypting** machines to keep orders secret and computing devices to **decrypt** them—these developments spurred the pace of technological innovation to levels never before seen.

## ADVANCING TECHNOLOGY

Many advancements in technology actually began before the start of the war. Although Germany's economy was in disarray at the end of World War I (1914–1918) as a result of the heavy reparations imposed by the Allies, the country had a top-notch pool of scientific and engineering talent. It had major companies that were involved in engineering vehicles and equipment, chemicals, and armaments. The Germans were excellent problem solvers, and they soon figured out ways to get around the restrictions on military rearmament imposed on them by the **Treaty of Versailles**. Because there were limits on the number of artillery pieces they could maintain, they set about devising ways to make the **munitions** delivered by that artillery more powerful and better controlled. They found loopholes in the treaty as well. Since rockets hadn't played a significant role in World War I, they were not mentioned in the restricted weaponry detailed in the treaty. Therefore, the Germans could expend effort on developing rocket-based missiles at will. Limited to a one-hundred-thousand-man army, they focused on technology in their initial drive to rebuild their military power. Eventually, they would violate the terms of the Treaty of Versailles altogether and set out unabashedly to conquer Europe. By then, however, the focus on technology was a key part of their military strategy.

Preparations were under way by the 1930s in Germany to give their forces the edge. This technological superiority embodied a feeling still common in the industrialized world that those nations that are more advanced technologically are superior to other nations. It fueled Germany's belief that they had a right to conquer other "inferior" nations. Germany and Japan both believed that their people were racially superior to the people of other countries in their respective regions. Because Japan was more technologically advanced than many of the less developed nations it **annexed** in Southeast Asia, it could hope to conquer its neighbors without developing radically new technologies. However, Germany's existing technology was not going to be enough to win the war in Europe.

It is no accident that Germany had a focus on science and technology. From the beginning, their goal was the complete domination of Europe. The problem was that Germany was not surrounded by simple island cultures. The other countries in Europe had steadily improved their weapons of war over centuries of warfare. The German government knew that in order to conquer those nations they needed new types of war machines, and Germany was determined to create them. Fed by anger at their country's treatment after World War I and led by the nationalist Nazi Party, the Germans intended to prove they were superior to the people of the countries that had defeated them.

## A MATTER OF TIME

Germany knew that it was going to invade Europe long before Europe knew it was going to be invaded. This gave Germany the opportunity to start on the development of new technologies well in advance. After England and France had agreed to let Germany annex the Sudetenland in Czechoslovakia in 1938 in the hope of preserving peace in Europe, the Germans expected them to let Germany continue to annex territory without challenge. They were not prepared for the swift change in Britain's position regarding German aggression in 1939. Faced with the imminence of war if Germany continued with its plans—which they intended to do—Hitler ordered Germany's top weapons inventors into top gear.

Personnel in the code-breaking project at Bletchley Park decrypt German communiqués.

Working feverishly, the government of Nazi Germany—and the Allies in response—provided scientists with funding and research facilities that they would never have been granted in peacetime. The German goal was to create machines and tools of unprecedented power to ensure their goal of world domination: rocket missiles; faster, larger planes capable of delivering more bombs; and a super-powerful bomb to deliver. In contrast, Britain's goal was to protect itself against future militarist incursions from Germany or other nations. They also developed technologies, such as radar, that were designed to detect enemy activity, as well as automated means of decrypting German communiqués. All the major players in World War II had scientists and engineers working on new ideas, but the Germans were unquestionably at the forefront of completing working versions and getting them into the field.

## A NEW KIND OF WAR

The scientific advances—and the scientists—of the war fueled an unprecedented period of technological innovation after the war. When Nazi Germany fell, the Allies—especially the Americans and Russians who invaded Berlin—recovered massive amounts of papers and records documenting the technologies the Nazis had been working on, as well as practical prototypes. Among this material was information on the jet engine, rocket science, and the atom bomb. The German scientists and engineers who surrendered or were captured held the key to these technologies. These scientists had been members of the Nazi Party who had

At the end of the war, many German scientists were captured by or surrendered to the US military.

supported or condoned the action of the Nazis. They had turned a blind eye to the use of slave labor to build their devices and the armaments used by Germany in the war. However, in the 1950s the United States was faced with a new and powerful enemy, the Soviet Union (USSR). Communism was a political philosophy directly opposed to the capitalism practiced in the United States and most of Western Europe. Under communism, everything was supposedly collectively owned. Individual wealth was not allowed, although in practice those at the top of the Communist Party prospered more than other citizens. The communist Soviet Union had retained control of most of Eastern Europe after World War II, giving it a large power base. The government of the United States feared that the Soviets, like Germany before them, would attempt to impose their views on the rest of the world. Knowing that their most powerful opposition was the United States, the USSR would naturally try to destroy it. Therefore, the US government considered it imperative to maintain military superiority to deter an attack by the Soviet Union—and military superiority meant scientific superiority. Faced with the need for the knowledge the Nazi scientists possessed, the government erased records of the scientists' participation in the Nazi Party and brought them to the United States. After debriefing them, it set them up in facilities where they could continue their research, this time for the benefit of the United States.

The postwar period was characterized by a new arms race—the United States and Russia both creating ever more powerful weapons to deter the other from attacking. Thus, a culture of "mutually assured destruction" was born. Government propaganda on both sides convinced the populations of the opposing countries that those on the other side of the **Iron Curtain** were their enemies, intent on their destruction. Naturally, this only further spurred them to continue scientific and technological advances. It was not merely a matter of practicality but also a matter of pride to outdo the other side. World War II and the continued improvements to the technologies born from it changed every aspect of life in the later twentieth century, and we still see the effects in the twenty-first century.

To understand the significance of the technologies developed during World War II, it is necessary to understand the actions and relationships of the participants in the war. Therefore, Chapter 1 describes the major events that occurred during the war. Chapter 2 discusses the situations and problems that countries on both sides needed to overcome. It clarifies how the events of the war created a need for new technologies and describes three technologies that were invented to address those needs: jet planes, rockets, and the computer. Chapters 3, 4, and 5 explain the development of those technologies in detail and discuss the effects that each invention had on the war. Chapter 6 is concerned with the effects those inventions had in the 1940s and in the years that followed the end of the war. Chapter 7 describes the lasting effects that those inventions of World War II still have on our lives today.

Adolf Hitler's public appearances were designed to inspire national pride among the German people.

CHAPTER ONE

# Inside World War II

At the end of World War I, the victorious Allied powers imposed harsh penalties on Germany, including paying for damages caused by the war and admitting to starting the war. The huge amount of money demanded, along with the destruction in Germany caused by the war, crippled the German economy, and the demand by the Allies that Germany take responsibility for the war offended German pride. It was not long before problems arose and led to one of the deadliest wars of the twentieth century.

## GERMANY AFTER WORLD WAR I

After World War I, the **kaiser** was forced to **abdicate**, and a democratic government was instituted. With the people angry and the country in chaos, the National Socialist German Workers

(Nazi) Party rose to prominence. Under the leadership of Adolf Hitler, the party appealed to the pride of the German people. It reassured them that Germans were descended from a "master race" and that it was Germany's destiny to rule the world. To achieve this dominance, they sought to purge Germany of any people they thought were not ethnically pure, such as the Jews. They also planned to annex parts of countries that contained large German populations, and rule over the rest. Throughout the 1920s, membership in the Nazi Party increased, and the party gained an ever-greater proportion of seats in the Reichstag, the German parliament. In the 1932 election for president, Hitler lost to Field Marshal Paul von Hindenburg, but he received 35 percent of the vote, and Nazi candidates won many local elections.

The government of Germany in the early 1930s was weak and ineffective, causing great dissatisfaction among powerful German politicians, industrialists, and businessmen. They eventually pressured Hindenburg into appointing Hitler **chancellor** of Germany. Initially, Hitler headed a **coalition** government composed of the many factions in the Reichstag. When it became clear that the coalition couldn't function effectively, Hitler, as head of the government, called for the Reichstag to be dissolved and new elections held. The Nazi Party gained the largest number of seats of any faction in the 1933 election but did not have a majority. To gain control of the government, on March 23, 1933, Hitler put up the Enabling Act for a vote by the Reichstag. The act gave Hitler and his cabinet the power to enact laws for four years without presenting them to the Reichstag. The act passed, and Hitler and the Nazi Party assumed control of the German government. Among other actions, Hitler began the rearmament of Germany.

Between 1935 and 1936, Italy, ruled by a dictator named Benito Mussolini, invaded and conquered Ethiopia. Shortly thereafter, Hitler signed a treaty with Mussolini. The treaty guaranteed cooperation between the two countries, both of which had the goal of territorial conquest, and the Axis was formed. Japan, ruled by Emperor Hirohito, also had territorial ambitions and wanted to take over nations in Southeast Asia and the Pacific. Less than a month after signing the treaty with the Italians, Germany signed the Anti-Comintern Pact with Japan. Through the pact, the countries agreed to work together to protect each other against the Soviet Union and communism. In July 1937, Japan invaded China and began the war in the Pacific.

One of the tenets of the Nazi government was that Germany had the right to "reclaim" territories from other countries that contained significant German populations. In line with this position, in March 1938, Germany annexed Austria and forced the chancellor to resign. They continued the plan to reclaim "German" lands by setting their sights on the Sudetenland, part of Czechoslovakia. Hoping that if they placated Germany they could avoid war, Great Britain and France signed the Munich Agreement with Germany and Italy in September 1938. This allowed Germany to annex the Sudetenland. A mere six months later,

Germany violated the Munich Agreement by moving farther into Czechoslovakia and occupying the country, creating the German Protectorate of Bohemia and Moravia. Germany then turned its attention to Poland. Increasingly nervous about Germany's aggression, Great Britain and France agreed to protect Poland.

German troops cross the River San during the invasion of Poland in 1939.

## A NEW WAR

To avoid having to fight too many enemies, in 1939 Germany signed the Molotov-Ribbentrop Pact. In this pact, Germany and the Soviet Union agreed not to attack each other—an agreement that Germany later violated. In September, Germany invaded eastern Poland, capturing it and the capital city of Warsaw. The Germans soon walled in an area of Warsaw to create the Warsaw Ghetto, in which they imprisoned Jews from throughout Poland. They later built a number of concentration camps in Poland to which they transported Jews from Germany and conquered countries to be killed or used as slave labor. Great Britain and France responded to the invasion of Poland by declaring war on Germany on September 3, 1939. World War II had begun.

In May 1940, Germany invaded Belgium, the Netherlands, and Luxembourg. By the end of May, Germany was in control of all three countries. Next it attacked France. In June, France signed a truce with the Germans. Under the terms of the agreement, Germany occupied the northern half of the country, including the Atlantic coastline, which gave them a strategic area from which to attack Great Britain. In southern France, a **collaborationist** government was established at Vichy. This government voluntarily supported the Germans.

After the fall of France, Great Britain and the British Commonwealth of Nations were the only forces fighting the Germans. It seemed as if Germany might succeed in conquering Europe. To make matters worse, in September the Germans' Axis partner Italy invaded Egypt, which was at that time controlled by Britain. One of the goals of the Axis offensive in North Africa was to control the flow of oil from the Middle East, which was necessary for the British to sustain their war effort. Now the British and the British Commonwealth of Nations were fighting in Europe and North Africa.

If they were to conquer Britain, the Germans needed to neutralize the British Air Force, especially the fighter command. Therefore, in June 1940, the German Air Force, called the Luftwaffe, began a massive bombing campaign that targeted Royal Air Force (RAF) airfields and facilities. They also struck factories that produced aircraft and aircraft parts. When this failed to subdue the British, they began bombing political and historical sites in London and engaging in mass terror bombing attacks. This huge bombing attack was called "the Blitz," which means "lightning." The Germans had planned to follow the air strikes with an invasion by sea, but when they were unable to destroy the British air forces, they were forced to abandon their plans.

In September 1940, Germany, Japan, and Italy signed the Tripartite Pact. This pact formalized the Axis. The main purpose of the pact was to **intimidate** the United States, which was neutral at that time, by making it look as if there would be a huge combined force facing them if they joined the war. The Axis knew that if America joined the war in support of the British it would be much harder for Germany to succeed in conquering Britain.

## CHANGING THE COURSE OF THE WAR

The Italians were having trouble in North Africa, and in February 1941 Germany sent the Afrika Korps to North Africa to reinforce the Italian troops. With the exception of the attempt to conquer Britain, the Axis powers had been remarkably successful. However, two events were to change the course of the war. First, in 1941, Germany launched an invasion of the Soviet Union. This ill-conceived move meant that Germany was now fighting a war on two fronts—against the British on the **western front** and the Soviets on the **eastern front**. At first, the invasion of the Soviet Union went well, with the Germans swiftly taking the Baltic states of Latvia, Lithuania, and Estonia. They then laid siege to Leningrad (now St. Petersburg). The Germans, moving deep into the heart of the Soviet Union, began to march on Moscow. The Soviets attacked the invading forces and drove them back. The second event that turned around the course of the war occurred on December 7, 1941, when the Japanese air force bombed the American naval fleet stationed at Pearl Harbor, Hawaii. The attack was supposed to destroy America's navy and air forces, making it impossible for them to enter the war. It had the opposite effect. The attack so angered the Americans that, on December 8, the United States declared war on Japan and began a major manufacturing effort to produce planes and armaments. On December 11, the Axis powers, in turn, declared war on the United States. In 1942, American forces joined the British, and the combined forces began a massive bombing campaign against Germany that lasted until the end of the war in 1945.

Meanwhile, the Japanese had succeeded in conquering the Philippines, Vietnam, Laos, Cambodia, and Singapore by the end of 1941. However, in June 1942, combined British and US forces stopped the Japanese navy from advancing further in the Battle of Midway.

In October 1942, British forces definitively defeated the Germans and Italians in Egypt at El Alamein, forcing them to retreat. The Americans and British followed this up by landing troops on the beaches of Morocco and Algeria in the part of North Africa controlled by the French. When the Vichy French troops failed to stop the Allied advance across North Africa, Germany occupied southern France. In May 1943, the Allies forced the last Axis troops in Tunisia to surrender, which ended the war in North Africa.

From August to November 1942, US troops fought the Japanese, who were attempting to conquer the Pacific Rim and advance toward Australia. The Americans finally defeated the Japanese at Guadalcanal in the Solomon Islands.

## THE WAR ON THE WESTERN FRONT

Meanwhile, in June 1942, Germany began a new offensive against the Soviet Union. The Germans attacked Stalingrad (now Volgograd) on the Volga River then proceeded to capture the Crimean Peninsula. However, the two-front war stretched

German resources thin. The war on the eastern front dragged into the winter months, and the Germans were now deep in the Soviet Union. German supplies had to come from Hungary and Romania, and the Soviets cut the German supply lines. Joseph Stalin, the dictator who ruled the Soviet Union, embarked on a campaign to defeat the invading German forces. He sent line after line of soldiers against them, relying on the huge population of the Soviet Union to gradually destroy the Germans by **attrition**. Running out of supplies and without **reinforcements**, the German invading forces surrendered in 1943.

## SUBDUING ITALY

Using the North African coast as a jumping-off point, in July 1943, the United States and Britain invaded the island of Sicily. By 1943, both the people and many in the government of Italy were disillusioned with the war and Italian losses. The invasion of Sicily meant that the Allies were now close enough to invade mainland Italy, and Allied bombings had destroyed much of the Italians' manufacturing capacity and caused a shortage of food. The **Grand Council of Fascism** met for the first time since the start of the war and voted to replace Mussolini with the previous ruler, King Victor Emmanuel III. The king assumed power, had Mussolini arrested, and appointed Italian Marshal Pietro Badoglio to form a new government, which surrendered to the Allies on September 8. The Germans responded by taking over Rome and northern Italy and freeing Mussolini from prison. They reestablished a puppet government in Italy under

During the D-Day invasion of Normandy, vast quantities of troops, vehicles, and equipment landed on French beaches.

Mussolini; however, the German control was short-lived. On September 9, Allied troops landed at Salerno, and in January more troops landed at Anzio, near Rome. On June 4, 1944,

the Allies liberated Rome. Control of northern Italy put them in a position from which they could fly bombers into eastern Germany.

In June 1944, the British, Americans, and Canadians launched Operation Overlord, landing troops on five beaches of Normandy, France, with the goal of liberating France. The massive invasion included 155,000 troops, 11,500 aircraft, 7,000 naval craft, 1,000 tanks, and tens of thousands of other vehicles. The fight against the Germans was difficult, but by the middle of August, Allied troops surrounded and decimated the German troops in Normandy.

On August 25, Free French forces liberated Paris. Over the next six months, the Allied forces freed most of France and Belgium and the southern part of the Netherlands. In December 1944, as the Allies attempted to advance into Germany, the Germans embarked on a final offensive, called the Battle of the Bulge. The goal of the campaign was to split the Allied forces in northern France. Several hundred thousand German troops and hundreds of German tanks attacked through the Ardennes Forest in eastern Belgium.

## Attack on England

The Normandy invasion would mark the turning point in the European theater of the war. The Germans would not surrender easily, however. In retaliation for the invasion, beginning on June 12, 1944, they

A London street in the aftermath of bombing by the German Luftwaffe, which caused massive destruction

began an intensive attack on England, using weapons they had been developing since the 1930s. These weapons included jet-powered flying rocket bombs. Hundreds of these missiles, called V-1s, were launched day after day from launchers on the French and Belgian coasts. Carrying 2,000 pounds (907 kilograms) of explosives, they appeared shrieking in the sky shortly before impact. They exploded with an incredible force capable of destroying multiple buildings. Faced with the destruction and death wreaked by "robot bombs" that could strike without being dropped by bombers, the British government evacuated a million people from London.

The Allies responded to the German missiles with a technological advance of their own—radar combined with ground-based antiaircraft artillery guns. The detection system used radar dishes that emitted pulses of microwaves (radio waves can also be used) that bounced off the missiles they encountered in the atmosphere. The signal from the returning wave was picked up by an antenna, allowing the location of the unseen missile to be identified. Antiaircraft artillery could then shoot down the missile before it achieved impact. (Today's radar can detect incoming aircraft and missiles from thousands of miles away.) These are only two of the technologies invented during World War II.

Thousands of American troops, fighting in bitter cold, halted the German advance, forced them to retreat, and then moved toward Germany. By the end of March 1945, all the Allied armies had reached the east side of the Rhine River in Germany. In May, the Americans and Soviets marched into Berlin from the east and west, respectively, and the Germans surrendered.

## ENDING THE PACIFIC WAR

At the end of May 1945, US troops captured the Japanese island of Okinawa. However, this was not enough to make the Japanese surrender. In the face of Japan's determination to keep fighting, President Harry Truman ordered the dropping of two atomic bombs on the cities of Hiroshima and Nagasaki. This resulted in the unconditional surrender of the Japanese on September 2, 1945, thus ending World War II. Estimates of casualties over the six years of the war range from 45 to 85 million people. It was the largest war in history.

## THE SECRET WAR

While soldiers, sailors, and airmen fought with weapons on the field of battle, a second war was being waged behind the scenes. The Germans—and subsequently the Allies—realized that the key to winning this war was not going to be guns but technology. It would be necessary to develop weapons that outclassed any seen before to successfully conquer—or defend—the modern world. This behind-the-scenes research and the resulting inventions led to advances not only in weapons but in technologies that would ultimately affect communications, computation, materials, transportation, and energy. Following the end of the war, many German scientists who had worked on scientific projects were brought to the United States to fuel its efforts to develop new technologies.

Although the roots of many of these technologies date back to World War I or even earlier, the need to obtain a technological advantage in World War II dramatically sped up efforts to realize the potential of these inventions. Science and math played a greater role in World War II than in any other war, and the new understanding of physics and mathematics opened up a world of inventions in the postwar world, which is still changing the way we live today.

From a De Haviland BE2 that was used as an early bomber, airmen dropped bombs by hand.

CHAPTER TWO

# The Technology of War

In the period between World War I and World War II, technology was advancing at a slow, steady pace. World War II brought about vast leaps in scientific understanding and the application of those principles to produce practical devices. This rapid advance was fueled by a race between Germany and the Allies to produce weapons to incapacitate the other side. Many of the devices invented, such as ballistic missiles and the atom bomb, changed the face of war forever. Others, such as jet planes, radar, rockets, computers, plastic **prosthetic** limbs, and modern antibiotics, changed the lives of people after the war in ways they never anticipated.

## THE FLYING WAR

Airplanes were used in World War I, but the war began only a decade after successful manned flight, which meant that the planes were still quite primitive—for example, biplanes made of canvas over a wooden frame. Air forces were small, and planes were limited to two roles: air-to-air combat and **reconnaissance** to discover information about the location and number of enemy forces. However, these early planes had to fly low and directly over the battlefields, so they were easy targets for enemy artillery. They were also hard to maneuver and made of much flimsier materials than modern planes. If they failed behind enemy lines, the pilot had little chance of escape. In addition, because flying

In World War I, biplanes were flown over battlefields to discover information about the enemy's troops.

was a new technology, there weren't yet trained pilots. The planes were built to be easy to fly, but the trade-off was that they weren't very maneuverable. Nonetheless, by the end of the war, they had become a significant part of the military **arsenal**.

Two important developments in airplanes took place during World War I. These later would have a big impact during World War II. The first was the addition of guns to the airplanes. These guns allowed the aircraft to take out artillery or other targets on the ground as well as the enemy's aircraft. The second advance was the creation of bombers. Bombers could be used to drop explosives on enemy targets, to destroy military equipment and factories making products for the war effort. This changed the strategy of war from merely fighting enemy forces to reducing the enemy's ability to fight. One of the roles played by fighter planes was to shoot down enemy bombers. Although airplanes played a merely supporting role in World War I, their contribution to the war effort led to an interest in building improved versions that could play an expanded role in future military encounters.

Between the wars, work continued on airplanes. Biplanes were replaced by metal-framed planes with a single pair of wings. However, the power for such planes was still provided in the same way—by a motor that turned a propeller, which created a stream of air under the plane to provide lift.

World War I had also established new relationships between countries. The Treaty of Versailles forbade Germany from rearming, but this did not stop Germany from working on new aeronautic, and other, military technology. It merely meant the Germans had to conduct much of their work in secret. They made a deal with the new, communist government of the Soviet Union to set up facilities there for the development of new weapons. In 1922, the German armament company Krupp set up a plant in southern Russia at Rostov-on-Don. That same year, the German aircraft company Junkers began to make airplanes in a town near Moscow, and Germany began training pilots for the soon-to-be-formed German air force at Lipetsk. In return for the Soviet-provided facilities, the Germans shared the fruits of their research. In addition to allowing Germany to prepare advanced technology for its next war, this relationship with the Soviet Union laid the foundation for the alliance between the Germans and Soviets at the start of World War II.

Britain also unwittingly fueled the future of German military aircraft technology by selling British aircraft designs to German companies building civilian aircraft. The Germans promptly set about modifying the designs in order to incorporate them into future military aircraft. Once Hitler came to power, the transfer of British technology ceased, but by then the Germans had incorporated the most up-to-date aircraft technology available into what would become World War II aircraft.

When Germany invaded Czechoslovakia in 1939, Hitler didn't expect that it would matter so much to the British government that they would declare war on Germany. Suddenly, the attempt to conquer continental Europe didn't seem like a walkover, and

German scientists were tasked with developing weapons that would be radically superior to those existing at the time. World War II was the first war in which the air power played as important a role as armies.

When the Germans embarked on their conquest of Europe, they conceived of themselves as unstoppable—and destined to win. Their strategy was to sweep across Europe in a massive military campaign that would overrun Western Europe before their targets could mount a successful defense. Indeed, in a remarkably short period of time, they succeeded in conquering the lowland countries of Belgium, the Netherlands, and Luxembourg, as well as France. When they reached the western coast of France and prepared to attack Britain, however, the situation changed.

The Battle of Britain, as the conflict was dubbed by Winston Churchill, was the precursor of modern warfare, in that planes in the air were as important as boots on the ground—perhaps more important. In every war since, aircraft has played a major role. In the summer and fall of 1940, the Germans launched everything they could from the air at Royal Air Force (RAF) targets in an attempt to destroy the British air force. Nonetheless, they were soundly defeated by the extremely effective British air defenses.

The Battle of Britain threw a spotlight on the weaknesses in the German military machine. Winning the war was going to require winning the air war, and achieving further victories would require faster and more powerful weapons. The Germans embarked on ambitious projects to produce faster planes by employing jet engines.

## Radar

It's impossible to discuss aircraft in World War II without including the major defense against them: radar. The widespread use of aircraft in World War II—especially as bombers—made it critical to find a way to

Soldiers operating a World War II radar system could detect incoming German aircraft.

detect them. If enemy aircraft could be identified before they reached their targets, they could be intercepted and shot down by fighter planes or antiaircraft guns before they could do damage.

Radar uses a system that produces short pulses of radio waves. When these waves hit a metal object, such as an airplane, they bounce back to a detector. The returning pulses are picked up by an antenna. The timing of the pulses is measured on a device called an oscilloscope, allowing the range to be determined. The direction of the antenna is used to determine the location of the plane. These two pieces of information in combination allow the operator to get a fix on the location of a plane or missile.

From 1934 to 1939, a number of countries independently developed radar systems, including Britain, the United States, Germany, the Soviet Union, Japan, France, and Italy. The system in Britain was designed by Sir Robert Alexander Watson-Watt, a Scottish scientist who had been working on using radio waves to detect storms. Working for the Air Ministry, he oversaw the installation of radar tracking stations along the east and south coasts of England in 1939. The information provided by his radar stations to the RAF was one of the major reasons that the British defeated the Germans in the Battle of Britain.

## ROCKETS

Rockets were not invented by the Germans; rather, they have a long history of military use. The Chinese learned how to make gunpowder in the first century CE by combining sulfur, saltpeter, and charcoal dust. In 1232, the Chinese were attacked by the Mongols. During the battle of Kai-fung-fu, the Chinese fired a barrage of gunpowder-powered bamboo rockets at the invaders. The gunpowder was ignited, and the gas that escaped from the open end of the bamboo tube shot the rocket forward as it exuded fire and smoke. The Chinese called these primitive rockets "arrows of fire." It's doubtful they did much damage, but they did intimidate the enemy. Eventually the Mongols also learned how to make rockets, and as they conquered much of Europe, they spread the technology.

By the end of the thirteenth century, the use of rockets was reported in Japan, Korea, India, and various European countries. From the thirteenth through the fifteenth centuries, many experiments were conducted with rockets. Roger Bacon (circa 1220–1292), an English monk, succeeded in creating better forms of gunpowder, which made it possible for rockets to go farther. Jean Froissart (ca. 1333–ca. 1400), a French historian, described in his *Chronicles* a method of launching rockets through tubes, which results in their traveling toward their target with greater accuracy. The French employed rockets in battle throughout the fifteenth century. They purportedly used them in 1492 in the defense of the city of Orleans led by Joan of Arc, and in several subsequent military actions. In 1540, Vannoccio Biringuccio

(1480–ca. 1539), an Italian metallurgist, wrote *De La Pirotechnia* (On Pyrotechnics). The book included chapters on making rockets for war and fireworks.

In the seventeenth century, several more books were published on the construction of rockets. Among these was a book on artillery and ballistics by an Austrian artillery officer named Conrad Haas (1509–1579), which describes the concept of multi-staging rockets. The first practical application of multi-staging was not military, however. In 1591, a German fireworks maker named Johann Schmidlap was seeking a way to make fireworks go higher when he invented the first practical multi-stage rocket. This rocket consisted of a large rocket (the first stage), which carried a smaller rocket into the sky. When the large rocket burned out, the smaller rocket ignited, moving higher in the sky. This is the principle used by multi-stage rockets today.

In 1687, the principles of modern rocketry were established when Sir Isaac Newton (1642–1727) published *Philosophiae Naturalis Principia Mathematica* (*Mathematical Principles of Natural Philosophy*). In this work, he laid out his "universal laws of motion." The third law of motion states that for every action there is an equal and opposite reaction, which is the basis for both jets and rocket **propulsion**. Newton also **espoused** the theory that if an object could be fired high enough and fast enough, it could escape Earth's gravity, and instead of falling to Earth, it would achieve orbit.

## The Father of Rocketry

Dr. Robert Goddard stands next to the first liquid-propelled rocket prior to launch.

It is generally acknowledged that "the father of modern rocketry" is American Robert Goddard (1882–1945). Goddard began designing rockets in 1912. He theorized that a small combustion chamber would be the most effective power source. In 1914, he patented designs for a rocket that used liquid fuel and a multi-stage solid-fuel rocket. While working at Clark University in Worcester, Massachusetts, in 1916, he wrote a paper on rocketry that was published in 1919 as a monograph by the Smithsonian Institution, under the title *A Method of Reaching Extreme Altitudes*. In this work, Goddard presented the mathematical basis for his theories of rocketry, described his experiments with solid-fuel rockets, and proposed that it was possible to travel beyond Earth's atmosphere.

Goddard demonstrated the first successful liquid-fueled rocket flight in 1926. He also invented a rocket-powered shell, which could be launched by a soldier. Although he successfully demonstrated it to the US Army in 1918, World War I ended shortly thereafter, so it was never used during that conflict. However, during World War II, it became the American bazooka. Many of Goddard's concepts were incorporated into the rocket-powered missile developed during World War II and into rocket science after the war.

## MODERN ARTILLERY WARFARE

In wars prior to World War II, the only way to deliver explosive munitions to the enemy was to haul them and the artillery to launch them to the battlefield. The explosive load—for example, the shells used in World War I—then had to be launched at the enemy. The distance a shell could travel was limited, so artillery had to be located fairly close to enemy lines. Once the bomber was invented, it could be used to drop explosives contained in bombs from the air. However, this incurred the risk that the plane delivering the bomb would be shot down. Distance was still a problem, as the range of planes in World Wars I and II was limited. The Germans conceived that an answer to these problems could be a bomb that flew by itself to the target. The first attempt at a rocket bomb was a surface-to-air missile called the Rheintochter (Rhine Maiden) after a character in Wagner's *Ring* cycle of operas. Work was started on it by the company Rheinmetall-Borsig. The first version used solid fuel for propulsion, but this was later changed to a liquid-fuel engine. This was a two-stage rocket; the first stage launched it from the ground, and when its fuel was exhausted, the second stage took over. Rheinmetall-Borsig was never able to get the missile to work properly, and the project was canceled in 1944. In 1943, Rheinmetall-Borsig had also begun work on a four-stage rocket-based missile called the Rheinbote (Rhine Messenger). The problem was that the Rheinbote required 4 tons (3.6 metric tons) of steel and burned 1,000 pounds (453.6 kg) of fuel, but it could only carry 44 pounds (20 kg) of explosive. Nonetheless, Hitler

Mechanical calculators like this were used for artillery calculations prior to the invention of the computer.

was captivated by this impressive four-stage rocket, and Germany used two hundred of them in its attack on the port of Antwerp in Belgium. However, the rockets caused only small amounts of damage, and because of the lack of a control system, they landed in random locations. Germany was determined to create rockets that could travel great distances to a target and deliver large **payloads** that could cause massive destruction, first on England and later farther afield in the United States.

## ENCRYPTION AND DECRYPTION

There were two motivations for the development of computers in World War II. The first was the need to perform rapid mathematical calculations for artillery trajectories and aiming. The increasing use of aircraft made this need more critical. These advanced calculations could be performed by hand on mechanical calculating machines by large numbers of operators, but it soon became clear that a better, automated approach was needed.

The second impetus was the Allies' need to break German codes. The Germans unquestionably had a powerful military machine, and the key to stopping it was learning where and when the Germans would attack. To this end, the Allies—in particular the British—intercepted German orders from the high command in Berlin to troops in the field. The problem was that these orders were encrypted and sent in code that the British couldn't interpret. The Germans used a machine called Enigma to encode their messages. The original Enigma machine had been invented in 1918 by Arthur Scherbius. Even though it was created during World War I, Scherbius was unable to interest the German military in his device, and in 1923, he formed his own company to manufacture it. The machine worked as follows: The operator pressed one of the twenty-six letter keys, which sent an electrical current to a circuit representing that key. The current then activated several rotors wired so that the letter was changed to another one. Each time the rotors were activated, a different replacement took place. In order to decode the message, a system was used at the receiving end to set the rotors to the same start position and then reproduce the series of contacts used in encoding it. No one who intercepted the message could read it because they couldn't reproduce the initial setup of the rotors and the subsequent changes. In 1928, the Poles got hold of an Enigma machine and examined the mechanism. As a result, the way it worked was known, but in Germany the machine was constantly being enhanced and more rotors added. Therefore, the number of possibilities for each letter was astronomical. The need to find a way to break the code resulted in pioneering work in computers. How the technical problems were solved and new technologies developed will be explored in detail in the following chapters.

The Messerschmitt was the first jet fighter plane used in World War II, and it ushered in the age of jet warplanes.

CHAPTER THREE

# Planes of War

Human beings have long been fascinated by the prospect of flight. Attempts to master the air date back to ancient times. Archytas (428–347 BCE), an ancient Greek philosopher, mathematician, and astronomer, is credited with having pioneered the use of mathematics for mechanics. Around 400 BCE, he built a bird-shaped model that was propelled through the air by a jet of steam and is reported to have flown 660 feet (200 meters). This is the first record of a self-propelled flying device.

In the Middle Ages, a number of experiments with flight took place using unpowered gliders. Two of those who engaged in such experiments were Abbas ibn Firnas (810–886 CE), an Arab inventor and physician living in Al-Andalus (part of modern-day Spain), and Eilmer of Malmesbury, a Benedictine monk at the

Malmesbury Abbey in Wiltshire, England, in the eleventh century. Both attached wings to their arms and leapt off buildings in an attempt to glide like a bird. They flew just a brief distance before crashing. Artist and inventor Leonardo da Vinci (1452–1519) designed a man-powered flying machine after studying birds' wings; however, his machine was never put to practical test.

## LEARNING TO FLY

The principles of modern flight were established by an English engineer, Sir George Cayley, sixth Baronet (1773–1857). In 1799, he developed the concept of the modern airplane with fixed wings and separate systems for lift, propulsion, and control. Cayley began building and flying models of fixed-wing aircraft in 1803, and in 1853, he built a glider capable of carrying a passenger. He wrote a three-part work on aeronautics called *On Aerial Navigation* (1809–1810).

Throughout the nineteenth century, various inventors experimented with ways to power gliders. None of these machines could be adequately controlled to allow a person to fly in them, however. Then, between 1867 and 1896, the German aviation pioneer Otto Lilienthal (1848–1896) developed a means of heavier-than-air flight. He designed and built various types of gliders and made numerous gliding flights. Many of the principles he applied to building successful gliders were later applied to powered aircraft.

## MILITARY FLIGHT

Brothers Orville (1871–1948) and Wilbur (1867–1912) Wright are credited with being the first to accomplish a human-powered heavier-than-air flight, in 1903. They continued to improve their craft, flying 24.5 miles (39.4 km) at Huffman Prairie in Ohio in October 1905. From the beginning of the invention of the airplane, the Wright brothers—and the US Army—saw its potential to provide a superior way of defending the country from the air. In 1905, the US Army attempted to negotiate a deal with the Wright brothers for the production of airplanes. However, an agreement was not reached until 1909. The Wright Military Flyer was purchased by the army and became the first military aircraft in the world.

The Wright brothers, pioneers in heavier-than-air flight, designed the earliest warplane.

It was only a few years later that World War I began. Airplanes were used in World War I to **strafe** targets on the ground and to bomb strategic enemy targets, but air forces were very small, and the range of the planes was limited. Most famous were fighter planes, which engaged in combat and attempted to shoot down enemy bombers and planes ferrying equipment and munitions. Enemy planes attempted to defend these targets, and the combat between planes was referred to as a "dogfight." In World War II, the role of the airplane would be greatly expanded.

## THE AIR WAR

From the beginning of World War II, Germany saw its air force, called the Luftwaffe, as a key component of military force. Germany relied on the Luftwaffe, especially its bombers, to subdue the countries it sought to conquer, and Hitler believed that one of the keys to winning the war would be air superiority. This turned out to be true, as the air battles of the latter part of the war played a major role in determining its outcome.

The key to air superiority was having the fastest aircraft. Therefore, Germany, England, and the United States all began efforts to develop jet-powered aircraft. Prior to this, aircraft had been powered mechanically by engines that rotated propellers. The turning propellers forced air back under the plane to lift and move it. This technology was far too slow to allow bombers to outrun the lighter, faster fighter planes or to allow planes to attack quickly and strike a distant target. Jet planes do not require propellers, relying instead on a jet of energy to propel the plane.

## The Principle of Jet Propulsion

The principle behind jet engines is that a force applied to an object results in an equal force being generated in the opposite direction. This is known as Newton's third law of motion. Jet engines work by shooting a jet of air backward, which thrusts an object forward. Technically, any engine that applies this principle could be considered a jet engine, including turbojet and rocket engines, for example. Usually, however, the term "jet" is used to refer to a type of aircraft engine that relies on a jet of air to produce forward motion. This technology improves significantly on the propeller-based approach because it produces much greater thrust.

In a jet engine, a mechanical device called a **turbine** rotates a **compressor**. The compressor pressurizes the air so that it is expelled as exhaust with great force. The turbine is powered by jet fuel. Air is pulled into the compressor, which pressurizes it as it spins. The fuel is mixed with the air and burned, and the exhaust from the process of combustion is discharged through a propelling nozzle. The nozzle constricts airflow then expands, shooting the exhaust out at high speed and propelling the plane. The force of the jet of exhaust is directed backward in order to force a plane to move forward.

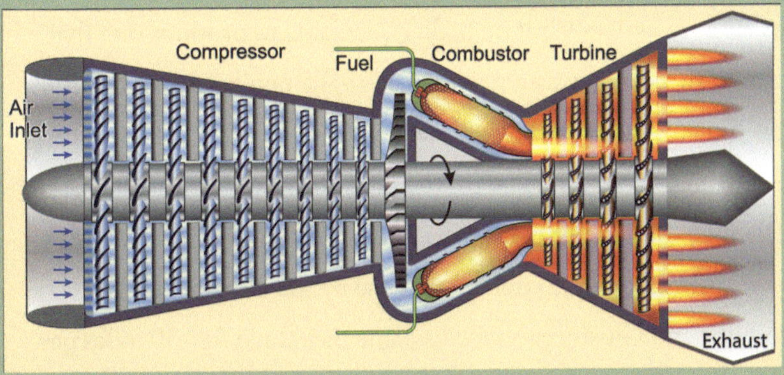


This diagram shows the components and operations of a turbine.

Jet engines allowed aircraft to move at much higher speeds. The fact that they generated more lifting power also meant airplanes could be larger.

## THE INVENTION OF THE JET ENGINE

The jet engine was invented by two engineers, a German and an Englishman, in 1939. In Germany, Hans von Ohain was a young physicist working for Dr. Ernst Heinkel, a German aircraft designer and member of the Nazi Party. Ohain developed the Henkel HeS 3, the first jet plane to actually fly. Another German engine designer, Anselm Franz, then took Ohain's design and modified it so that it was suitable for use in a warplane. He designed the famous German fighter plane, the Messerschmitt ME 262, which took to the air in 1944. It was the first fighter plane with a jet engine to fly in World War II.

While the Germans were developing their jet engines, an English RAF engineer named Frank Whittle developed his own jet engine. Whittle had actually been issued a patent on a jet engine as far back as 1930, but he hadn't been able to produce one that would successfully fly a plane. In 1939, he finally succeeded in producing a workable design, and in January 1940, the British Air Ministry contracted with the Gloster Aircraft Company to produce a jet fighter plane. The first planes produced by Gloster were primarily for homeland defense by the British. By 1942, Whittle and Gloster produced a plane that could fly 430 miles per hour (692 kilometers per hour) flying at 25,000 feet (7,620 m).

The new jet plane outperformed the best non-jet British fighter plane, the Spitfire. The success of the Gloster plane spurred other British engine companies to try to develop their own jet planes, and by 1943, Rolls-Royce had taken over production of the engines for the British jet fighters.

Although the Germans got their jet planes into the air before the British, they lacked minerals like cobalt needed to make strong metal alloys for the blades of turbines, and the Germans' jet engine design was more complicated than Whittle's. As a result, the German engines would often last only 10 to 25 hours before burning out, whereas the engines in the British planes could run for 150 hours. The design of the engines continued to improve throughout the war. Rolls-Royce eventually sold some of its engines to the Soviets, who used them in their MiG-15 jet fighters. The Americans built their first jet engine at General Electric after Britain shared Whittle's technology. The first American jet fighter plane was the Bell-XP-59.

## THE ROLE OF JETS

Jet planes were primarily used for aerial plane-on-plane combat. Jet aircraft were faster than propeller-powered fighter planes, but they were harder to control, and their range was limited because they consumed so much fuel. However, after the war, the technology opened up an entirely new era in aeronautics. The Messerschmitt was superior to the Allied fighters in speed and armament. In addition to the Messerschmitt, the Germans flew the Henkel He 162 and Arado 234. The planes were used

An American B-29 Super Fortress bomber flies over Nakajima Aircraft Company in Japan in 1945.

for bombing and reconnaissance as well as for attacking other planes. One issue with the new planes was that their great speed affected the accuracy of the shots fired by the mounted guns. This resulted in a need to change the way fighters maneuvered. Instead of approaching head-on while firing, the planes needed to engage in large dipping maneuvers to slow the planes before firing. The Gloster Meteor planes were primarily used by the Allies for defense against the German fighters and for reconnaissance. Late in the war, the Japanese developed the Yokosuka MXY7. This was a jet rocket plane that was flown by **kamikaze** pilots directly into Allied ships in order to sink them.

The Allies used jet bombers to carry out massive attacks on Germany toward the end of the war. These attacks destroyed the facilities Germany relied on to manufacture armaments and fuel. On the Pacific front, huge B-29 jet bombers were employed to drop atomic bombs on the Japanese cities of Hiroshima and Nagasaki. The horrific destruction caused by the atomic bomb resulted in Japan's surrender. By the end of the war, the slow, clunky planes introduced in World War I had become sleek, fast, and large. Fighters and bombers were transformed into highly effective weapon systems. Since World War II, jet planes have become the backbone of military forces around the world.

A V-2 rocket, having been moved into place, is prepared for launching.

CHAPTER FOUR

# Rockets

Rockets were introduced to European military forces during the late eighteenth century, after Indian forces used rockets against the British troops in British-controlled India. British artillery expert Colonel William Congreve (1772–1828) designed rockets for the British side. The Congreve rockets were highly effective, and in the War of 1812, they were used against the Americans at Fort McHenry—these are the rockets referred to in “the rockets’ red glare” in “The Star-Spangled Banner.” Rockets at this time did not cause great damage, however. They had to be fired in very large quantities to be effective. When **breech-loading** canons that launched exploding shells were introduced during the Franco-Prussian War (1870–1871), that type of artillery replaced rockets. However, they would resurface again in twentieth- and twenty-first-century warfare.

## ROCKETS IN WORLD WAR II

Modern rocketry was pioneered in Nazi Germany. One of the developers of rocketry was Hermann Oberth (1894–1989). A physicist and engineer, in 1922 he wrote a doctoral dissertation in which he described rocket flight into outer space. When his dissertation was rejected, he privately published it, and in 1929, he expanded it into a full-length book called *Wege zur Raumschiffahrt* (*Ways to Spaceflight*). His work caught the imaginations of engineers around the world and resulted in the formation of many rocket societies. In Germany, Oberth mentored amateur rocket designers (called rocketeers) in one such society, the Verein fur Raumschiffahrt (Society for Space Travel).

In 1937, Germany began the Aggregate Rocket Program in Peenemünde on the Baltic Sea. Oberth was among the German engineers and scientists who participated in the project. Under the direction of Wernher von Braun (1912–1977), a German rocket engineer, this program enabled Germany to produce a series of progressively more advanced rockets, which played a key role their military strategy. The most famous rockets developed at Peenemünde were the V series. These rockets all started with V (V-1, V-2, etc.). The "V" stood for *Vergeltungswaffen*, which translates as "weapons of retaliation or vengeance."

## THE V-1 ROCKET

The first of these rockets was the V-1 flying bomb. The V-1 rocket was the first cruise missile—a missile that could be ejected by a plane and fly automatically. Known to the Allies as "the buzz

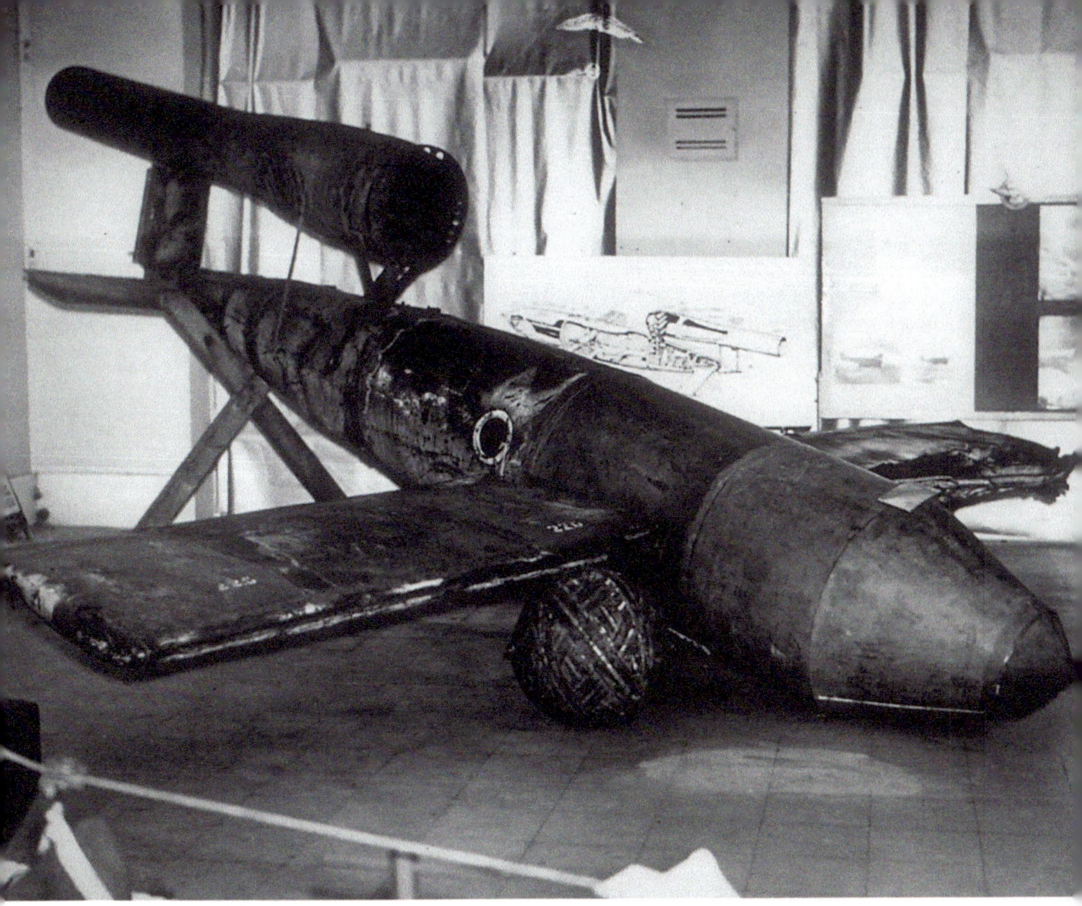

The V-1 rocket guided missile made it possible to deliver explosives without dropping bombs from planes.

bomb" because of its distinctive sound, or as the "doodlebug," the V-1 was used during the bombings of London and southern England. In June 1944, prompted by the successful Allied landings in Europe in 1943, the Germans launched the first V-1s against southeast England. They were fired from the French coast, which was under German control. A V-1 rocket carried about 2,000 pounds (907 kg) of explosives. The rockets flew in a specific direction, but couldn't be targeted to hit an exact spot. Therefore, V-1s were primarily used for mass bombing and were designed

## Wernher von Braun

More than any other scientist, Wernher von Braun is associated with the development of rocket technology. He was the son of Baron Magnus von Braun. Fascinated with rocket science, in 1933, at the age

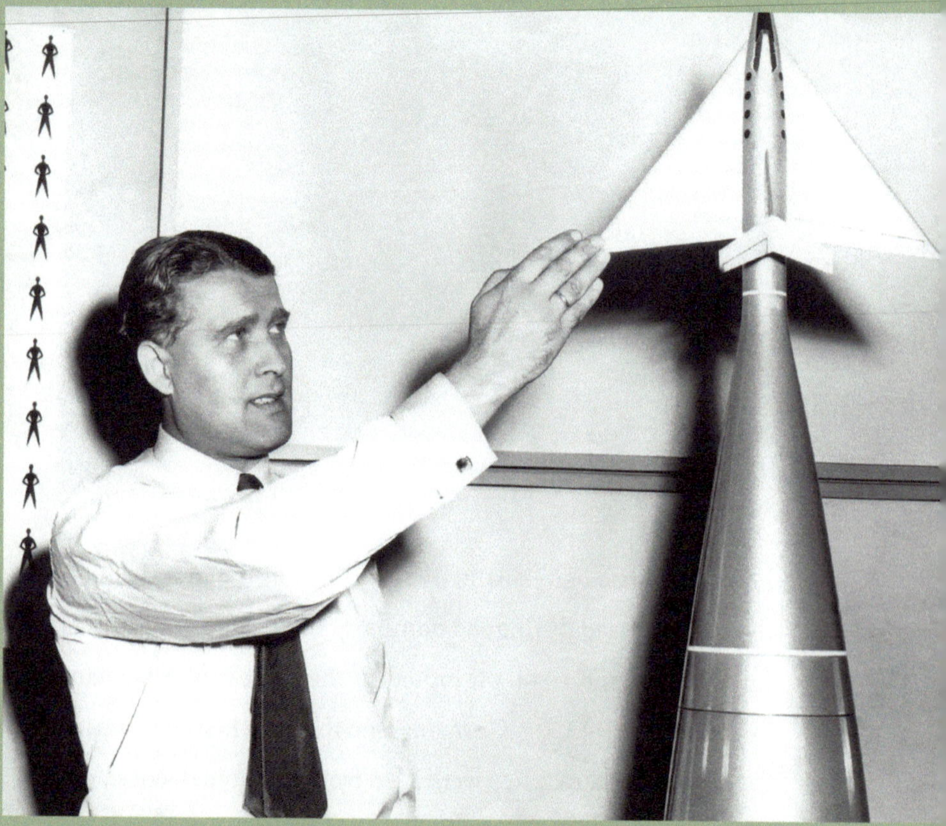

Wernher von Braun shows a model of one of the rockets he has designed.

of twenty-one, he joined the German Army artillery division under Dr. Walter Dornberger. This division was charged with building rockets and would eventually be moved to Peenemünde. Braun played a lead role in the development of the V-1 and V-2 rockets.

Once the power of the rockets was apparent, Adolph Hitler put the project under the control of the military production committee of the Ministry of Armaments and War Production. Eventually, the Gestapo (Nazi secret police) tried to take control of the promising project, and place SS (Schutzstaffel; Nazi Defense Corps) General Hans Kammler in charge. In 1944, in an attempt to oust Braun, the head of the Gestapo, Heinrich Himmler, "invited" Braun to give up the V-2 project. Braun refused, and three days later he was arrested by the Gestapo and thrown in prison. Charges were leveled against Braun stating that he was not interested in the war effort but in using the V-2 for space travel. He was also accused of being a British sympathizer with a plan to escape to England. Major General Dr. Walter Robert Dornberger intervened by going directly to Hitler and claiming that Braun was critical to the project. The charges were dropped and Braun resumed work on German rockets.

to produce random destruction and terrorize populations. The top speed of the V-1 was 390 miles per hour (627.6 kmh), so the British were able to destroy many of the rockets with antiaircraft artillery and weapons mounted on fighter jets.

## THE V-2 ROCKET

The V-2 rocket was the first ballistic missile, a missile that could travel a distance before dropping to hit its target. It used an automatic pilot consisting of two electric gyroscopes that guided a set of four external steering vanes to stabilize the rockets' motion. Work on the V-2 rocket began as early as 1936, and tests of versions of the rocket were being conducted by 1939. Under the direction of Wernher von Braun, testing of the V-2 began in the spring of 1942 at Peenemünde. The first two tests failed. In the third, however, the rocket flew 120 miles (193 km) and reached an altitude of 50 feet (15.2 m). In 1943, the Allies bombed the facility at Peenemünde. Subsequently, production of the V-2 was moved to an underground complex at Mittelwerk, near Nordhausen in the Harz Mountains. The manufacturing plant was building about nine hundred missiles per month by the end of the war.

V-2s were used in combat for the first time on September 6, 1944, when they were fired toward Paris. Attacks on England and Belgium with V-2 missiles also started in September 1944. It was not long before the Allied troops caught on to this new missile and wanted to put an end to it. Because the Germans believed that fixed launch sites would be vulnerable to Allied attacks, the V-2 was deployed mainly from a vehicle called a Meillerwagen.

This was a portable erector/trailer. The missile lay in a horizontal cradle, which could be raised to a vertical position for launch. Once the launch platform was in position, the vehicle itself could be detached and moved away. It changed the tide of warfare with its effectiveness and destruction.

## ROCKETRY IN OTHER COUNTRIES

Germany wasn't the only country to recognize the utility of rockets in military applications. The Soviets created the Jet Propulsion Research Institute in 1933 to research liquid-fuelled ballistic missiles. They succeeded in launching a rocket-based missile in 1937. Shortly afterward, Soviet dictator Joseph Stalin, determined to wipe out any members of opposing parties who might challenge his position, executed Marshal Tukhachevsky, a prominent leader of the Bolshevik Party who was also a patron of the institute. He then had the head and deputy head of the institute executed and the head engineers imprisoned, which put an end to rocket research in the Soviet Union. Japan was interested in rocket development but lacked the industrial infrastructure of Germany and the Soviet Union. They concentrated solely on air-to-air missiles. They developed the Igo-1-A and Igo-1-B radio-controlled cruise missiles. Production on these missiles started late in the war, and they were never used in combat. The British produced an antiaircraft radio-controlled rocket-based surface-to-air missile, called the Stooge, which was specifically designed to shoot down Japanese kamikaze planes attacking naval ships. They also developed some small short-range missiles, which were used by the navy during the invasion of Italy. During the war, the United States used Robert Goddard's research on solid-fuel missiles to develop the handheld bazooka, a surface-to-air missile that could be launched by soldiers in the field. None of these efforts came close to the advanced rockets developed in Germany.

## ROCKET ATTACKS ON ENGLAND

Rockets played a major role in the Nazis' attempt to subdue England. They used both V-1 and V-2 missiles to wreak havoc on London and southern England. At the height of the attack, over one hundred rockets rained down daily on England. The numbers of rockets fired gradually decreased as the Allied forces attacked and destroyed German rocket sites, but by the time the last site was captured by the Allies in October 1944, seven thousand to nine thousand rockets had hit England. Subsequently, the Germans also used the rockets against the port of Antwerp and other Belgian targets. Initially the rockets were fired from sites in France, Belgium, and the Netherlands. By late 1944, the Allies had captured the French and Belgian sites, leaving the Germans to launch most of the V-2 missiles from a site near the Hague in the Netherlands. The final launch site was captured by the Allies in March 1945. In response to losing their missile-launching sites in France and Belgium, the Germans developed a prototype of a winged V-2. They hoped this version would be able to glide to its final destination. However, the war ended before a successful production version could be developed.

The Allies invaded Germany in the spring of 1945. As the Soviet Army approached Peenemünde, Braun and his staff, fearing the Soviets' reputation for cruelty, fled. He acquired counterfeit documents and eventually got many of his team to Austria, where he surrendered to the US Forty-Fourth Infantry Division. Braun was on the US government's list of key scientists, and he was recruited to work for the United States under a program that would come to be known as Operation Paperclip. Under the auspices of the project, the US Joint Intelligence Objectives Agency created false employment histories and removed evidence of Nazi Party membership from the records of scientists deemed desirable so that they could be granted security clearances and work in the United States. Braun worked for many years for the US Army on rocket development. During the Korean War, he led the rocket development team at the Redstone Arsenal in Huntsville, Alabama. When the National Aeronautics and Space Agency (NASA) was established in 1958, he because director of the Marshall Space Flight Center in Huntsville, where he developed the Saturn-V rocket. He remained director until 1970, when he left NASA and joined Fairchild, an aerospace engineering company in Germantown, Maryland, as vice president for engineering and development. In 1977, he died of cancer.

The Enigma machine was a mechanical device used to encrypt messages.

CHAPTER FIVE

# The Computer

Computers are first and foremost machines that perform mathematical calculations. Since the earliest civilizations, people have sought faster and easier ways to compute. This mechanism would undergo many changes during its evolution, and would play an especially key role in the fate of World War II.

## THE HISTORY OF COMPUTERS

While there were instances of computing devices as far back as Ancient Greece, practical advances did not come until the Middle Ages. During this time, inventors were creating mechanical devices to calculate the positions of planets. In 1642, Blaise Pascal (1623–1662), a French mathematician, invented a machine that used a series of gears and could perform all four arithmetic operations: adding, subtracting, multiplying, and dividing.

In 1673, Gottfried Wilhelm Leibniz (1646–1716) constructed the first of many Stepped Reckoners, which used a drum, which was turned by hand, to rotate a series of gears in set increments to perform the four arithmetical operations. Leibniz's design formed the basis of calculating devices for the next 275 years.

In order for calculating machines to evolve into computers, a method to program them had to be created. Joseph-Marie Jacquard (1752–1834), inventor of the Jacquard loom, supplied that method. In 1801, he created a system of punch cards that would control the operations of devices such as looms, mechanical calculators and counting machines, mechanical organs, and the like. The cards were fed into a "reader" on the device, and the location of the holes punched in the cards controlled the movements of various parts of the machine. This is similar to the technology by which holes punched in player piano rolls cause an automated piano to play music.

The idea for the first true mechanical computer was conceived by Charles Babbage (1791–1871) in 1822 and eventually dubbed the Difference Engine. It was designed to calculate polynomial equations (equations used to find the values of multiple unknown quantities). The first computer program was written by Augusta Ada King, Countess of Lovelace (1815–1852), an English mathematician, to run Babbage's computer. Babbage worked on various versions of the Difference Engine throughout the mid-1800s. These inventions laid the foundations for the work done on computers during World War II.

## ENIGMA

The German military sent orders to their forces by radio in code. The key to the Allied success against Germany was breaking that code. British intelligence had access to intercepted German messages, but they were not able to decode them. In 1919, the British government had set up a code-breaking facility in London called the Government Code and Cipher School. During World War II, this agency was based at an estate called Bletchley Park in Buckinghamshire and staffed by mathematicians and others who were adept at working with codes and puzzles. The intelligence-gathering and code-breaking project was codenamed Ultra.

The code used by the Germans was generated by a series of electro-mechanical cipher machines produced under the brand name Enigma. An Enigma machine had several rotors, or cylinders. Letters were chosen and then the cylinders rotated and produced random letters to replace them, encoding a message. It was nearly impossible to break the code because there were so many possible arrangements of letters, and the series of letters was always different. The only way for the receiver to decode the message was to mirror the exact series of rotations of cylinders performed by the original machine. In 1938, the Poles captured an Enigma machine. Early Enigma machines used three cylinders. Every German message began with a series of letters, repeated twice, that indicated the original start position of the cylinders. For example, the code might be XXYXXY. The code itself was encrypted, however, so it appeared as ABQDLF. Using the clue of the three-letter code, the Poles figured out a way to decode German messages. When they learned of German plans to invade Poland in 1939, they sent the captured Enigma machine and their notes to British Intelligence.

However, the Germans were continually upgrading the Enigma machines, adding rotors and making the code more complex. By 1939, Enigmas could be set up $1.5 \times 10^{19}$ ways, and in 1941, the Germans produced a new version to communicate with U-boats (German submarines). The 1941 version of Enigma could encode messages $1.8 \times 10^{20}$ different ways.

One of those who played a key role in breaking the Engima code was Alan Turing, a mathematician at Cambridge University. Turing was interested in the idea of machines that could perform logical functions. He had designed a hypothetical machine that could be given rules that it could use to manipulate symbols on a strip of paper—that is, it could be programmed. These rules, called algorithms today, are the same types of procedures today's computers use to perform their functions. The "Turing Machine" was a simple forerunner of the modern computer.

At Bletchley Park, Turing designed an electromechanical device called the British Bombe that reproduced the action of the Enigma machine. The contract to build it was awarded to the British Tabulating Company, and it was built under the direction of an engineer, Harold Keen. Eventually multiple bombes were built. Each one was about 7 feet (2.1 m) wide, 6 feet 6 inches (1.98 m) tall, and 2 feet (0.61 m) deep, and each weighed about a ton (0.9 t).

This is the British Bombe designed by Alan Turing to decrypt German communications encrypted using Enigma machines.

Drums were mounted on the front of each bombe in three groups of twelve vertical triplets. Each triplet corresponded to the three rotors of an Enigma scrambler. The rotation of the drums was automated by means of an electrical circuit. The bombe could run through all the possible positions to which a rotor could be set in about twenty minutes. In 1942, the British shared the design of the decoding equipment with the United States, which built its own decoding bombes.

In order to set the bombes to decode messages, the team needed to identify repeated phrases, such as the weather report that appeared at the beginning of each message sent. Such phrases were called a "crib," from which the bombe could electrically test all the possible combinations of encoded letters and decode messages. Under Turing's direction, the bombe simplified the work of breaking the German codes and eventually allowed the British and their allies to learn of Germany's plans and respond accordingly.

## THE LORENZ CIPHER

In 1941, the Germans began using an encoding attachment for teleprinters. Teleprinters were machines into which messages could be typed and sent over telephone lines, then reproduced on the other end. They were used by the Germans to send encrypted messages to their strategic command posts. The most commonly used machines were the Lorenz SZ40/42 (and later the SZ42A and SZ42B), which could transmit wirelessly, and the resulting code was called the Lorenz cipher. The machines were used frequently, starting in 1942, to send communications between the

## Alan Turing

Alan Turing (1912–1954) is considered by many to be the father of computer science. He studied at Cambridge University in England and Princeton University in the United States. At twenty-four years old, he published a paper explaining "computable numbers." In the paper, Turing described many of the concepts for developing computers. In 1937, he designed (but didn't build) "the Turing Machine," a computing device that could manipulate symbols on a strip of paper in the same way that an electronic computer algorithm works today. His work at Bletchley Park was pivotal to the Allied success in World War II.

After the war, he joined the National Physical Laboratory, where he created one of the earliest designs for a stored-program computer, called the Automated Computing Engine, or ACE. He then went on to Manchester University, where he worked on some of the earliest programmable computers. He is known also for developing the "Turing Test," which states that a computer can only be considered "intelligent" if a human being interacting with it can't tell that he or she is dealing with a computer. In 1952, he was arrested for being homosexual, which was still illegal in England at that time. Two years later he died of cyanide poisoning a few days before he turned forty-two. An inquest ruled his death suicide. In 2009, the British government apologized publically for his treatment.

German High Command in Berlin and German Army command posts throughout Europe. Messages from the Lorenz machines were captured by the British and sent to Bletchley Park. The development of the Colossus computers made it possible to automate decryption of the messages.

## COLOSSUS

Mechanical "computers" are analog devices, which means they use physical components such as gears to perform their calculations. These gears typically reach a certain point then cause another gear to move, thus engaging in a physical "counting" process. In contrast, digital computers represent numbers symbolically, using digital "pulses" of "on" or "off" electrical current. Numbers are represented as a series of 1s and 0s (indicated by the on/off state of the electric current), and mathematical operations can be performed on them. The final number is printed out in its decimal equivalent on a computer monitor or printer.

The Colossus computers were electronic digital computers that were controlled by a program. They were designed by British engineer Tommy Flowers, and were used for cryptanalysis at Bletchley Park from 1943 to 1945. Their major use was decrypting the flow of messages from the Lorenz machines. This information was particularly important because it contained high-level strategic intelligence. The first Colossus, the Mark 1, was placed in operation in December 1943. The second, more advanced version, the Mark 2, was used for the first time in June 1944. By the end of the war, ten Colossus machines were in use, revealing vast amounts of information about Germany's strategic plans.

One of the differences between Enigma and Colossus was that Enigma was electromechanical; Colossus was completely electronic. Enigma relied on mechanical rotors to decrypt information, but all of Colossus's processing was done digitally, the same way that computers today operate. Unlike computers today, Colossus was huge and had very little internal memory. It used vacuum tubes rather than the tiny transistors used in modern computers, and it was programmed externally by setting plugs and switches. It could not perform multiple functions as computers now do. It was designed for a single purpose—to decrypt coded messages. Nonetheless, this primitive mechanism signaled the beginning of the computer age.

After the war, commercial airlines started using jet airplanes built with technology developed during the war.

CHAPTER SIX

# Aftermath of the War

The end of World War II was the beginning of a technology boom, as the inventions developed for war were adapted to new applications. That boom was particularly pronounced in the United States. After the war, all the countries in Europe—winners and losers—had to recover from massive destruction to their infrastructure and industries. The United States was a different story. Except for Hawaii and the Aleutian Islands off the coast of Alaska—both attacked by the Japanese—it had not been the victim of direct bombing attacks and could put its resources toward developing advanced technologies.

## JET PLANES

The technology developed for jet engines during World War II would change the face of both warfare and peacetime travel.

After the surrender of Germany in 1945, the Americans gave the information they uncovered on German jet technology to engine companies Pratt & Whitney and General Electric. This new information allowed Pratt & Whitney to solve the problem of massive fuel consumption by jet planes by building planes that used two engines instead of one. In 1948, they designed the first twin-engine jet. The improved jet engines made it possible to build jet-powered bombers. The first was the B-45 Tornado, put into service in 1948 and used in the Korean War (1950–1953).

It wasn't long before the new jet technology was used for civilian applications. Sir Geoffrey De Havilland (1882–1965) was an English aircraft designer and founder of the De Havilland Aircraft Company. During the war, De Havilland had designed fighter planes for the British. In 1949, he built the first jet airliner, the De Havilland Comet. The jet engine allowed airplanes to climb higher and faster than older propeller planes. The Comet could travel 480 miles per hour (772 kmh) and radically reduced travel time. The British Overseas Aircraft Corporation (BOAC) used the De Havilland Comet to begin the first commercial jet airplane service in 1952, flying from London to Johannesburg, South Africa. The planes had problems, however. The aluminum alloys used in their construction suffered from metal fatigue when exposed to repeated pressurization and depressurization. After several crashes in 1953 and 1954, the entire fleet was grounded.

It took four years for De Havilland to design and recertify an improved version of the Comet. During this period, US aircraft manufacturers Douglas and Boeing produced their own jet planes and came to dominate the industry. Boeing's jet was the 707 and Douglas's the DC-8. In the 1950s and 1960s, aircraft manufacturers began using turbofan airplanes, which is the technology still used for jet planes today.

## ROCKETS

After the war, German rocket-based missile technology and the scientists who worked on it were used by the US government in two ways: to develop advanced missile technology and to achieve manned spaceflight.

One of the German rockets that was designed at Peenemünde close to the end of the war was the Wasserfall Ferngelenkte Flakrakete (the Waterfall Remote-Controlled antiaircraft rocket). This was a surface-to-air missile designed to shoot down aircraft. It was similar to the V-2 rocket but considerably smaller—only one-quarter the size. It was steered to its target by remote radio control after being launched. Radar was used to track its target, and a transponder on the missile sent signals back to its controllers so its location could be tracked. An operator could guide the blip representing the missile on a radar screen toward the blip representing the target plane—until the blips merged. Later the missile was modified to pick up its target's radar signal directly. It carried 660 pounds (300 kg) of liquid explosive. When it hit its target, it created such a large explosion that it took out a number of planes. Design on the missile started in 1941, and test flights were begun in 1943. However, successful flight was not achieved until

## The Cold War

The Cold War was a period of political hostility between the United States and the Soviet Union. The Cold War began at the end of World War II and lasted until the fall of communism in the Soviet Union in 1991. During World War II, the United States implemented the

The dropping of atomic bombs on Hiroshima and Nagasaki ended the war but started the nuclear arms race.

Manhattan Project to develop an atomic bomb. Through espionage, the Soviets discovered information from the Manhattan Project, and in 1949 they tested their first atomic bomb.

The postwar period was characterized by an arms race. The governments of the United States and the Soviet Union each feared that they would be vulnerable to attack if the other side had superior weaponry. They also believed that if they were able to retaliate in a devastating way, this would discourage the other side from attacking. Thus, a culture of "mutually assured destruction" was born. In an atmosphere of mutual distrust, people lived in constant fear that the Cold War would erupt into a full-blown nuclear war. This stress affected the political interaction between the two countries and their allies for fifty years, leading to a culture of psychological warfare, propaganda, and espionage on both sides. It also colored the daily lives of citizens, and contributed to sociological changes. Books, movies, music, and art were influenced by the impending threat of nuclear doom as well. Although it was impractical to bomb each other, the two countries could engage in other types of competition, such as the space race. In an all-out effort to prove they were intellectually and technologically superior, the US and the USSR strove to be the first to accomplish key milestones such as orbiting Earth, putting a satellite in space, building a space station, and above all, being the first to land on the moon.

February 1945, shortly before Peenemünde was evacuated because of the Allied advance into Germany. Therefore, the Waterfall never saw action in the war, but the technical design contributed to US postwar missile development. Prototypes were captured by the Americans and the design became the Hermes A-1 Missile. New versions of the missile continued to be made until 1954, when development was halted because the project had failed to produce a missile that was ready for deployment in the field.

## THE FIRST MANNED ROCKET

The Germans foresaw the application of manned rockets as well as rocket-powered missiles. In a project codenamed Reichenberg, they developed a manned version of the V-1. It was designed to be a one-use rocket that would be piloted to a target and then destroy it, killing the pilot, much like the Japanese kamikaze planes. The 27-foot-long (8.2-meter-long) rocket had a cockpit that contained the flight instruments. Hanna Reitsch, a Nazi test pilot, flew the rocket on several tests flights. She found that its frame was subject to severe vibration and felt that too many pilots would be lost before reaching the targets. Because it was so late in the war, the problems could not be fixed before the war ended, so a piloted rocket was never flown during World War II.

## THE AMERICAN ROCKET DREAM

The US government was so convinced of the importance of rocket technology that it brought a number of Nazi scientists to the United States after the war. It established a rocket development project in Huntsville, Alabama, under the direction of the German scientist Wernher von Braun. Braun worked at the Fort Bliss Army Base in Texas until the Korean War began, when he was transferred to Huntsville, Alabama. From 1950 to 1956, he headed the army's rocket development team at Redstone Arsenal. There, he developed the rocket that was used in the first nuclear ballistic missile tests, and the first high-precision inertial guidance system for the missile. The rocket was dubbed the "Redstone Rocket." In the role of director of the Development Operations Division of the Army Ballistic Agency, Braun developed the Jupiter-C. Its design was based on the Redstone Rocket his team had developed.

On January 31, 1958, Braun began the United States' space program when the Jupiter-C rocket was used to launch the first US satellite, *Explorer 1*. The US government was more focused on the military applications of rockets than on putting rockets into outer space. Most of the work in that area was being done by the Soviet Union. Sergei Korolev (1907–1966), a senior Soviet rocket scientist, developed new rocket designs and initiated the Sputnik ("Satellite") program, which was designed to launch a satellite into space. In 1957, the Soviet Union launched *Sputnik 1*, the first satellite to be placed in a low Earth orbit. The success of *Sputnik 1* created the feeling in the United States that America was falling behind the Soviet Union technologically. There was widespread fear that if the Soviets controlled space, they would have a military advantage over the United States, which would endanger the country's security.

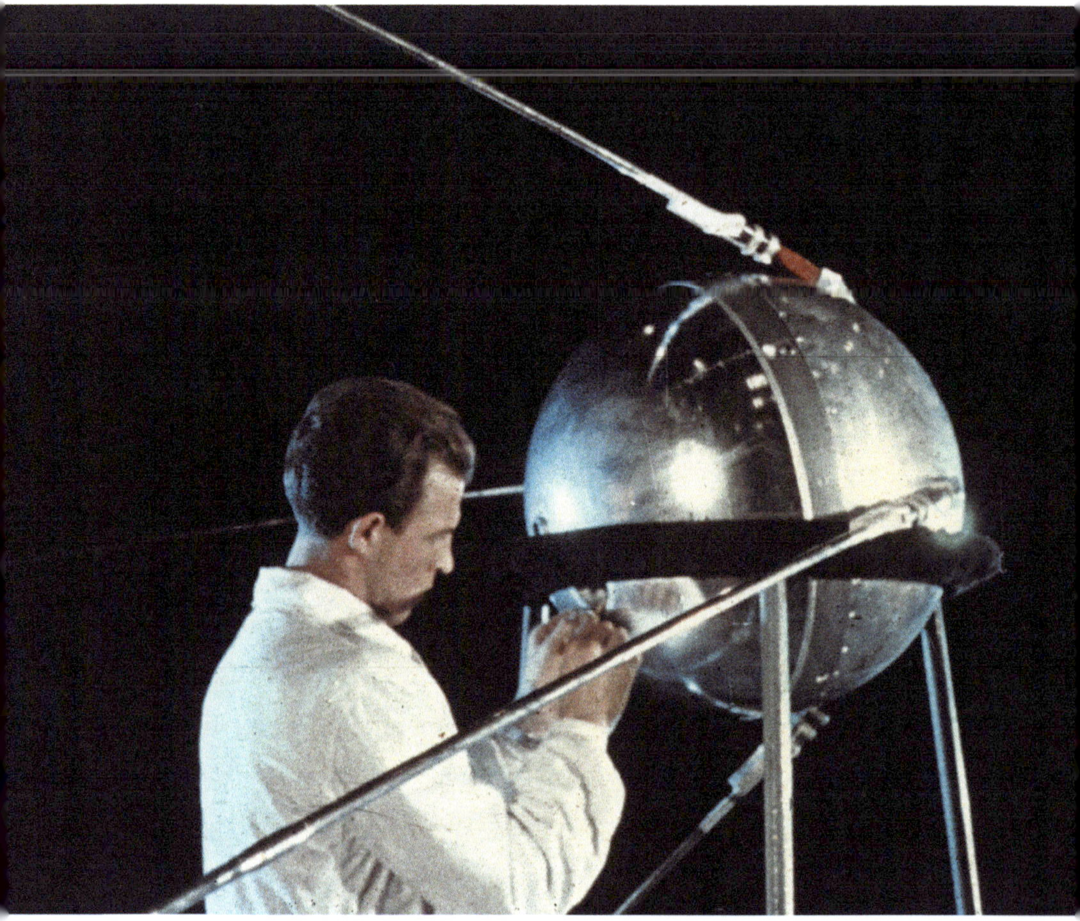

A Soviet scientist works on *Sputnik*, the first satellite launched into space.

At the time that *Sputnik* was launched, the United States had been working on a rocket called the Vanguard, which was intended to carry a satellite into space. These efforts had been unsuccessful, however, because of the unreliability of the launch system. Wernher von Braun had proposed in 1954 that he be allowed to design a launch vehicle, but the government wasn't interested.

Now they decided that he and his team should do so. In 1958, the National Aeronautics and Space Administration (NASA) was established. In 1960, the Marshall Space Flight Center was established at the Redstone Arsenal in Huntsville, Alabama. Braun became the center's director, a role he held until 1970.

On May 25, 1962, President John F. Kennedy told the American people that the United States would put a man on the moon within a decade. On July 20, 1969, Neil Armstrong became the first man to walk on the moon. Since then, space exploration has remained a constant.

## COMPUTERS

The British were not the only ones developing computer technology during the war. In 1939, John Vincent Atanasoff, an Iowa State College mathematics and physics professor, demonstrated proof conceptually that an electronic computing machine could work, and he received funds to build it. Working with his graduate student Cliff Berry, he built the Atanasoff-Berry computer, which was completed in 1942. This is considered the first digital computing machine, operating entirely electronically, without the need for mechanical calculating parts. However, because it was not programmable, many do not consider it to be a full-scale computer like Colossus. The Atanasoff-Berry computer was built to solve linear equations. Further development on the machine was abandoned when Atanasoff went on to World War II work. Nonetheless, Atanasoff and Berry laid the foundations of many elements of modern computers, including the use of binary arithmetic and electronic switching, which would play a major role in the development of digital computers in the postwar era.

In 1943, the US Navy asked the Massachusetts Institute of Technology (MIT) to build a flight simulator they could use to train bomber crews. The team at MIT built a large analog computer, but it turned out to be too inaccurate to be useful. Flight simulators would have to wait until the development of digital computers. Bell Labs had better luck with the Relay Interpreter. In 1943, the US Army asked the company if it could help in testing its M-9 Gun Director. A mathematician at Bell Labs, George Stibitz, created an electrical-relay-based calculating machine. It was programmable by paper tape and used 440 relays. The fact that it could be programmed to do specific types of calculations meant that it could be used for other purposes after the war was over. Another relay-based calculator was designed by Harvard professor Howard Aiken in 1944 and subsequently built by IBM. The Harvard Mark-I, as the machine was dubbed, took up an entire room. The machine was used to produce mathematical tables. All these computers had one thing in common—they were designed to perform one particular task.

Technicians work on ENIAC, the first programmable computer—which took up an entire room.

The ENIAC (Electronic Numerical Integrator and Computer) was completed in 1946 at the Moore School at the University of Pennsylvania. Unlike other early computers, which were designed to perform one type of calculation for a particular purpose, ENIAC was a general-purpose computer. What was remarkable about ENIAC is that it could be reprogrammed again and again to perform different tasks. The creators of ENIAC were John W. Mauchly and J. Presper Eckert Jr.

Prior to the invention of electronic computers, computations were done by human "computers." These specialists used mechanical calculating machines to solve lists of equations for applications such as aiming artillery on the battlefield. Although both men and women were hired as computers, the majority were female college graduates with degrees in mathematics. During the war, much of the male population was deployed overseas in the military, but women were available. They were also less expensive to employ than men and had superior dexterity. The answers they computed were compiled in tables and published for use in the field.

The Moore School of Engineering at the University of Pennsylvania in Philadelphia was one of the locations where these computers worked. A handful of highly trained women computers operated a machine called a "differential analyzer," which could calculate the path of a shell. Six women were chosen from among this group to be trained as programmers for ENIAC. By the time ENIAC was ready for programming, it was late in 1945 and World War II had ended. However, members of the US military had seen the Colossus computer at work in England and believed in the benefits of computers for future military operations. The military continued to support Mauchly and Eckert's project, and the six women programmers completed the first computer program, which ran on ENIAC in 1946. In its finished form, ENIAC occupied an entire 30 foot by 50 foot (9 m by 15 m) room. After ENIAC was placed under military control and taken to the Aberdeen Proving Ground in Aberdeen, Maryland, several of the women went on to careers as programmers for other organizations. Although ENIAC was developed to calculate trajectories for artillery, once it was transferred to Maryland, it was also used in the government's project to develop the atomic bomb.

The competition between the United States and the Soviet Union after the war continued to fuel the rapid development of improved technologies that had their roots in the science of World War II.

A prototype of the German delta-winged jet plane, whose design provided the basic concept for many later stealth aircraft

CHAPTER SEVEN

# Lasting Effects

Many of the technologies developed during World War II have had lasting effects on our way of life. They have changed not only the way wars are conducted but also the way we travel, work, communicate, and socialize.

## ENHANCING AIRCRAFT

Many of our most advanced aircraft have their roots in technologies developed in Nazi Germany. One such design is the delta-winged aircraft used by stealth fighters such as the F-16. This type of design was developed by two German brothers, Walter and Reimar Horten, during World War II. In order to test their design, they built the Ho-229, a delta-winged glider, which they tested in 1944. Then they turned the project over to the Gothaer Waggonfabrik

Company, where further development was done, including installing a jet engine. A twin-engined version of the delta-winged plane, the Ho-229 V3, was under construction in 1945, but the war ended before it could be finished. One of the Ho-229 gliders and the partially built twin-engine Ho-229 V3 were captured by the Americans during Operation Paperclip and sent to a man named John Northrop, along with captured design documents. Northrop, who had founded the Northrop Corporation to build planes in the 1930s, had experimented unsuccessfully with the idea of delta-winged planes in the 1920s. With the Nazi material, Northrop was able to start work on US delta-winged aircraft. He tested one successfully in 1948, but since the aircraft was propeller-driven, jet engine planes made it obsolete before it went into production. However, the concept behind the Horten brothers' design, which was aerodynamically efficient and hard to pick up on radar, formed the basis of stealth bombers used today.

During the war, a German engineer named Alexander Lippisch invented the concept of a **ramjet** delta-winged plane. His design used a standard turbine to get up to speed, then switched over to ramjet mode, in which it used the forward motion of the plane to collect and compress air. This design gave the plane great fuel efficiency. The German company Darmstadt Akaflieg designed a prototype, the Darmstadt D-33. After the Darmstadt Akaflieg factory was destroyed by bombing in 1944, the project was moved to another company, Munich Akaflieg. In 1945, the Americans discovered a prototype glider, renamed Darmstadt Akaflieg/

Munich Akaflieg DM-1. It was sent back to the United States, where it was examined by the National Advisory Committee for Aeronautics (the predecessor of NASA). Numerous modifications were made to the design, but Lippisch's work influenced various Convair delta fighter planes, including the XP-92, XF-92A, XFY, F2Y, F-102, and F-106. The XP-92 was the first US delta-winged fighter, and the F-102 Delta Dagger was used in the Vietnam War. The F2Y Sea Dart was a seaplane version, which took off from pontoon-like skis on the surface of the water. Research into delta-winged planes in Britain resulted in the development of the Handley Page HP-115, the Avro Vulcan bomber, and the Fairey Delta 2 (FD2). The FD2 was the first plane able to reach speeds in excess of 1,000 miles per hour (1,609 kmh).

The technical knowledge gained from designing these military planes, in turn, contributed to the development of the Concorde supersonic airliner, which was put into operation by Air France and British Airways in 1976. Able to fly from London to New York in three and a half hours, the Concorde was in service until 2003.

## NEW USES FOR SPACE

In the early 1970s, the *Mariner* spacecraft orbited and mapped the surface of Mars. Subsequently, the *Voyager* spacecraft orbited Jupiter and Saturn and sent back pictures of their surfaces and those of their moons, as well as Saturn's rings. This information significantly increased our knowledge of the planets. Also in the 1970s, the space station Skylab was built, allowing experiments to be conducted in space over an extended period. In 1981, the first

## Suborbital Aircraft

Another area in which German aircraft technology contributed to US aircraft development was suborbital aircraft. Eugen Sänger, a Czech engineer working for Germany, conceived of a suborbital aircraft that could circle the Earth in the stratosphere and deliver a load of bombs to a target on the other side. The German air ministry was interested in this idea because it would have allowed Germany to bomb the United States. Bombers in the 1940s did not have the necessary range for such a strike. Sänger's plane was called the Silver Bird. It was to be launched by a rocket sled that would carry it down a track at a speed of 1,200 miles per hour (1,931 kmh). The plane would fire its onboard rocket motors and accelerate to a height of 90 miles (145 km). Ultimately, it would achieve a speed of 13,700 mph (22,050 kmh). It would then move by bouncing in a series of hops between space and the upper atmosphere until it reached its destination. The idea was that it would drop its bombs on the United States and then land in the Pacific Ocean, where it would be retrieved by the Japanese. In 1942, the project was canceled by the Luftwaffe, which thought it was too bizarre, and calculations based on information discovered at the end of the war indicated that the plane would not have worked as designed. However, Sänger's design principles contributed to the development of the North American X-15 rocket plane, the X-20 Dyna-Soar, and the space shuttle.

space shuttle—the first reusable spacecraft—was launched. It was used to carry out a wide variety of experiments in space, and to place and repair satellites. There were twenty-four successful space shuttle missions before the tragic explosion of the space shuttle *Challenger* in 1986.

Much like the reconnaissance planes of World War II, satellites provided military information during the Gulf Wars. They were used to obtain information on the formation of enemy troops and their movements, and to provide warning of enemy missile attacks. In addition, they could provide navigational information when troops needed to move in the desert without landmarks. Satellites contributed significantly to the success of coalition forces in the Middle East.

The ability to travel to outer space and place satellites in orbit has changed many aspects of our lives, especially the way we communicate. By the 1970s, orbiting satellites were in common use. Much of the information we rely on today is tied to their use. Communications satellites receive a signal broadcast from Earth and relay it to receivers in homes and businesses around the world. Television, phone, radio, and the Internet all rely on communications satellites for wireless communication.

Meteorological satellites monitor weather and climatic conditions. They provide information on storms, snow cover, and ocean currents. They also track the dispersion of ash from volcanic eruptions and the spread of wildfires. Environmental monitoring satellites keep track of the hole in the ozone layer, changes in vegetation across Earth, the state of glaciers, and the spreading of oil spills. Surveillance satellites are used by US agencies charged with ensuring homeland security.

## THE AGE OF THE COMPUTER

No other device has changed people's lives as much as the computer. The smartphone you carry in your pocket today performs more functions than the first room-sized computers developed a mere seventy-five years ago. Today, computers play a role in every aspect of our work and personal lives. They run production lines in factories and are used to create animated movies. They make it possible to take instant pictures and videos—and share them with the world. They run medical equipment that saves lives in hospitals, and in tablet form they allow health-care professionals to record information in real time as it is gathered from patients. We can get a college or technical education by means of a computer. In addition, we use them to buy—and sell—every imaginable type of good and service.

The first computer to be used widely in commercial applications was the UNIVAC computer produced by the Remington Rand Corporation in 1951. Descendants of UNIVAC are still being sold today by Unisys Corporation. In 1953, IBM started selling its first computer, a mainframe computer called the 701. These early computers cost hundreds of thousands of dollars, and were bought primarily by large corporations and the government. Over the next three years, IBM sold nineteen of the computers. Their customers were research laboratories, aircraft

UNIVAC was the first widely used computer. It stored information on large reels of magnetic tape.

companies, and the US government, all organizations that needed to process large amounts of data. In 1954, IBM introduced the 650 magnetic drum calculator for "data processing." The magnetic drum used to store data was the predecessor of the hard drive used in today's computers. The 650 was the first computer to be mass-produced, and IBM sold 650 within a year.

Early computers used vacuum tubes to switch their electronic signals, and a large array of vacuum tubes took up a great deal of space. In 1947, three physicists—John Bardeen, Walter Brattain, and William Shockley—invented the transistor, a tiny electronic device that could perform the same function as a large vacuum tube. In 1956, researchers at MIT built the TX-0, the first computer to use transistors instead of vacuum tubes. In 1958, IBM began selling the 7000, the first commercially available transistorized computer. Transistors made it possible to reduce the footprint of computers. In 1965, Digital Equipment Corporation introduced the first minicomputer. In addition to being smaller than IBM's mainframe computer, it featured a monochrome cathode ray tube monitor, which allowed the computer to display the results of data processing instead of printing them out. It sold for $18,000, as opposed to over $100,000 for an IBM mainframe. For the first time, computers became affordable for small- and medium-sized businesses. In 1966, Hewlett-Packard entered the computer market with the HP-2115, which provided businesses with a computer with the same processing power as large mainframes. In addition, this computer could be programmed with a variety of different computer languages.

In 1971, John Blankenbaker produced the first personal computing device, the Kenbak-1. It had a 256-kilobyte memory and was programmed by a series of switches. He advertised it in *Scientific American* for $750, but made few sales. In 1974, Xerox Corporation created the Alto workstation. It incorporated a built-in mouse, could store several files at the same time, and provided menus and simple icons. Xerox never sold Alto as a commercial product, but it did give a number to universities, and some of its features were subsequently incorporated into new versions of computers. The electronics company Micro Instrumentation and Telemetry Systems (MITS) produced the first commercial microcomputer, the Altair 8800, in 1975, using Intel's 8080 processing chip. The Altair 8800 was featured on the cover of the January issue of *Popular Electronics*. Orders flooded into the company. Bill Gates and Paul Allen licensed BASIC as the software language for the Altair 8800. Ed Roberts, the engineer who invented the Altair 8800, coined the term "personal computer."

In 1973, IBM developed a personal computer prototype with a keyboard and small monochrome monitor. It started selling PCs in 1981. Bill Gates and Paul Allen had founded Microsoft Corporation in 1975 to generate programs and operating systems for personal computers. IBM contracted with Bill Gates to create the operating system for their PC. Gates got IBM to allow him to retain the rights to the disk operating system (DOS) because they saw PCs as merely a niche market. Gates earned millions of dollars from licensing DOS and then went on to develop the first Microsoft Windows operating system in 1983.

In 1976, Steve Wozniak designed a simple computer for hobbyists, the Apple I. He and his friend Steve Jobs started Apple Computer, and a year later, they produced a user-friendly personal computer, the Apple II. The Apple II had to be hooked up to a television, which served as its monitor. Unlike previous personal computers, it could show colored graphics if it was hooked up to a color TV. Millions of Apple IIs were sold. In 1983, Apple launched its first personal computer with a graphical user interface that featured easy-to-recognize icons, which made it easy for ordinary

The first Apple computer was one of the first desktop computers. Many early desktop computers were sold to hobbyists. No one anticipated their widespread public use.

people to use. Computers have continued to get progressively smaller, moving from desktop to laptop to tablet computers.

By the 1980s computers had already become an important tool for military and government applications. The US Department of Defense Research Agency (DARPA) sought to build a distributed network of computers that could continue to communicate with each other in the event of a military attack. They came up with a network of computers called ARPANET, which connected computer networks at various academic and government research facilities. Funding from the National Science Foundation and private funding for commercial backbones resulted in worldwide participation in the new "network of networks," known as the Internet. In the early 1990s, the government opened up the Internet for commercial and personal use. As a result, millions of people and companies all over the world connected to share information and conduct commercial transactions. In 1989, British computer scientist Tim Berners-Lee invented the World Wide Web, a collection of documents written in a language called Hypertext Markup Language (HTML). The language allows the creators of the documents to insert links to other documents. Users are able to embed pictures, videos, and other components that are rendered in a web browser. The computer has come a long way since then. Today, computers can be as small as your hand—existing as smartphones and able to be carried in your pocket.

The legacy of World War II continues to affect our lives—and will continue to have an impact on future generations. Inventions such as computers, communications satellites, the Internet, rockets, and jet planes all have their roots in World War II. On one hand, these technologies have made the world a smaller place. They've made it easier for people in distant lands to see how others live and understand what they have in common. They fuel cultural exchange and mutual understanding. They also provide a powerful tool for oppressed people to publicize their plight and to resist tyranny. On the other, they have put powerful weapons in the form of new planes, missiles, and bombs into the arsenals of nations around the world. It is up to us to decide how these technologies will be used in the future.

# GLOSSARY

**abdicate** To give up the throne.

**Allied powers** The countries united against Germany in World War II. These included the United States, Great Britain, France, the USSR, and China.

**annex** To attach; to make part of another country.

**arsenal** A collection of weapons.

**artillery** A large movable gun that fires bullets, shells, or missiles (such as a canon or antiaircraft gun).

**attrition** A gradual decrease in size or number.

**Axis powers** The countries united against the Allied powers in World War II. These included Germany, Italy, and Japan.

**breech-loading** Describing a weapon into which a shell or cartridge is inserted from the rear, like today's guns, rather than from the front, like a musket.

**chancellor** The head of the German government (much like a prime minister).

**coalition** A group of different parties that agree to work together.

**collaborationist** Describing a person or group that cooperates with the enemy.

**compressor** A device that uses pressure to make a large volume of a substance, such as air, fit in a smaller space.

**decrypt** To put a coded message back into its original form.

**eastern front** The battleground in Europe to the east of Germany.

**encrypt** To put in code.

**espouse** To embrace as a cause or political position.

**Grand Council of Fascism** The political organization to which Mussolini belonged, which ruled Italy during World War II.

**intimidate** To make a person or group of people afraid.

**Iron Curtain** The barrier to communication with the United States and Western European countries imposed through censorship and secrecy by the Soviet Union on its people and those of the Eastern European countries it controlled.

**kaiser** The hereditary ruler of Germany.

**kamikaze** A Japanese pilot who destroyed enemy ships by crashing into them.

**munitions** Military arms and ammunition.

**payload** The material that a bomb carries, such as explosives or nuclear material.

**propulsion** The force that moves a plane forward.

**prosthetic** An artificial limb.

**ramjet** A type of jet engine that relies on a stream of fuel injected into a moving stream of air that is exhausted out the rear of the plane to move it forward.

**reconnaissance** Gathering data about the formation and movement of enemy troops.

**reinforcements** Additional troops sent to help a military unit in the field.

**strafe** To shoot bullets from plane-mounted guns at targets on the ground.

**Treaty of Versailles** A treaty signed by Germany, the United States, and the major European countries after World War I in which Germany agreed to disarm, take responsibility for the war, and pay for damages caused by the war.

**turbine** A type of motor that consists of vanes or blades that are moved by fluid or air passing over them.

**western front** The battleground in Europe to the west of Germany.

# BIBLIOGRAPHY

Computer History Museum. "Timeline of Computer History." Retrieved August 6, 2015. http://www.computerhistory.org/timeline.

Editors of the Encyclopedia Britannica. "Wernher von Braun." *Encyclopedia Britannica*. Retrieved August 6, 2015. http://www.britannica.com/biography/Wernher-von-Braun.

Eljet. "Jet Aircraft of World War II." Retrieved August 6, 2015. www.ellejet.com/jet-aircraft-of-world-war-ii.php.

Encyclopedia of Science. "History of Rocketry." Retrieved August 6, 2015. http://www.daviddarling.info/encyclopedia/R/rocketry_history.html.

Ford, Brian J. *Secret Weapons: Technology, Science & the Race to Win World War II*. Oxford, England: Osprey Publishing Company, 2011.

Gavrieli, Kfir, Nora Salim, and Armando Yañez. "The Jet Engine: A Historical Introduction: The Development of the Jet Engine During World War II." Stanford University, March 16, 2004. Retrieved August 6, 2015. http://cs.stanford.edu/people/eroberts/courses/ww2/projects/jet-airplanes/planes.html.

History.com Staff. "Battle of Britain." 2009. Retrieved August 6, 2015. www.history.com/topics/world-war-ii/battle-of-britain.

———. "World War II History." 2009. Retrieved May 24, 2015 http://www.history.com/topics/world-war-ii/world-war-ii-history.

Jackson, Kenneth T. "World War II." The Gilder Lehrman Institute of American History. http://www.gilderlehrman.org/history-by-era/great-depression-and-world-war-ii-1929-1945/world-war-ii.

Kopplin, John. "An Illustrated History of Computers." Kent State University, 2002. Retrieved August 6, 2015. http://www.cs.kent.edu/~rothstei/10051/History.htm

Lethbridge, Cliff. "History of Rocketry." *Spaceline*. Retrieved August 6, 2015. http://www.spaceline.org/history/1.html.

Mindell, David. "Learn NC: The Science and Technology of World War II." University of North Carolina. Retrieved August 6, 2015. http://www.learnnc.org/lp/editions/nchist-worldwar/6002.

NASA. "Brief History of Rockets." Retrieved August 6, 2015. http://www.grc.nasa.gov/www/k-12/TRC/Rockets/history_of_rockets.html.

National World War II Museum, The. "WWII Overview." Retrieved August 6, 2015. http://www.nationalww2museum.org/learn/education/for-students/ww2-history/overview.html.

Shactman, Tom. *Terrors and Marvels: How Science and Technology Changed the Character and Outcome of World War II*. New York: William Morrow, 2002.

Smithsonian National Air and Space Museum. "Military Use of the Airplane." Retrieved August 6, 2015. http://airandspace.si.edu/exhibitions/wright-brothers/online/age/1910/military.cfm.

Stamp, Jimmy. "The History of Rocket Science." *Smithsonian Magazine*. February, 2013. Retrieved August 6, 2015. http://www.smithsonianmag.com/innovation/the-history-of-rocket-science-4078981/?no-ist.

Taylor, John W. R. "Military Aircraft." *Encyclopedia Britannica*. Retrieved August 6, 2015. http://www.britannica.com/technology/military-aircraft.

United States Holocaust Memorial Museum. "World War II: Timeline." *Holocaust Encyclopedia*. Retrieved August 6, 2015. http://www.ushmm.org/wlc/en/article.php?ModuleId=10007306.

University of Pennsylvania School of Engineering and Applied Science. "ENIAC: Celebrating Penn Engineering History." Retrieved August 6, 2015. http://www.seas.upenn.edu/about-seas/eniac.

# FURTHER INFORMATION

## Websites

**The History Learning Site: World War II**

www.historylearningsite.co.uk/world-war-two

This website details the history of World War II.

**NASA: A Pictorial History of Rockets**

www.nasa.gov/pdf/153410main_Rockets_History.pdf

This website explores the history of rockets using various pictures and descriptions.

## Videos

**Crash Course: World War II**

www.youtube.com/watch?v=Q78COTwT7nE

A brief animated lesson discusses the causes and effects of World War II.

**The Creation of the Computer**

topdocumentaryfilms.com/creation-computer

A History Channel documentary recounts the history of the computer.

**Secret Stories of World War II**

www.youtube.com/watch?v=itn_i1YVwwU

A National Geographic documentary tells untold stories from the war.

# INDEX

Page numbers in **boldface** are illustrations. Entries in **boldface** are glossary terms.

# ABOUT THE AUTHOR

**Jeri Freedman** has a Bachelor of Arts from Harvard University. She worked for a number of years in the education department of the Anti-Defamation League in programs providing information on the Holocaust to history teachers. She then worked for fifteen years at high-technology companies. She is the author of more than forty young adult nonfiction books, including *A Documentary History of the Holocaust: The Warsaw Ghetto and Uprising*, *Robots through History*, and *Airborne Commandos* (Special Ops series).